Contents

Any words appearing in the text in bold, **like this**, are explained in the Glossary.

Living together

Life is tough, but it gets easier if you have a little help from your friends. Living together is often safer than living alone. Animals that live together can help each other find food, make homes and keep warm in winter.

Usually the things that live together belong to the same **species**, but sometimes two or more quite different species share their lives. One species may steal something from the other one, and give nothing back. That makes it a **parasite**. Other species are real partners, with each helping the other. This kind of arrangement is called **symbiosis**.

The sea anemones clinging to this hermit crab get extra food from whatever the crab catches and leaves. In return they defend the crab from its enemies with their painful stings.

Small birds like these greenfinches and bramblings often team up to look for food in winter, but they live apart in summer.

Short and long partnerships

Many symbiotic partnerships do not last long. Different species come together, take whatever they need from each other, then split up. The mixed flocks of small birds that search for food together in winter are like this. They help each other watch out for danger as they feed, so staying in a flock makes good sense. But, for the rest of the year, they can manage quite well on their own.

Other species form symbiotic partnerships for life. They never split up, and if they did, they would soon be in deep trouble. For example, many animals cannot **digest** their food without the help of tiny **microbes** that live in their stomachs, and the microbes can live nowhere else. These partners must stay together to survive.

Smart birds

Some birds have learned to team up with other animals to find food. One of the best examples of such birds is the black-throated honeyguide, which lives in African forests. The honeyguide eats the waxy honeycombs made by wild bees. As the honeyguide is not strong enough to break into the bees' nests itself, it gets help.

Its favourite partner is an African honey badger. The badger has strong teeth and claws, and it loves honey. The honeyguide dances in front of it, making a chattering call, then flies off a little way. The badger understands this is a sign, and follows. The honeyguide keeps leading the badger until they get to the nest. Then the badger breaks into it and enjoys a feast of honey, while the bird eats the honeycomb.

This honey badger will have no trouble breaking into a wild bees' nest, but it needs a honeyguide (inset) to show it where to find one.

Bird and human partnerships

Honeyguides also lead humans to bees' nests. Africans have used them, just like the honey badger does, for thousands of years. Another long-lasting partnership between birds and humans features the barn owl, which hunts small **mammals** over grassland. When humans began to cut down trees to create farmland, barn owls had many more places to hunt. The owls also discovered that farm buildings such as barns made ideal places to nest. Old-style farmers still use barns for storing the grain they harvest from their crops. They like barn owls nesting in their barns because the owls catch and eat lots of rats and mice that would eat the grain.

The barn owl nests in a barn, and repays the farmer by catching rats and mice to feed her fluffy chicks.

Pestpickers

Many big **mammals** that feed on the grasslands of Africa are attacked by tiny creatures, such as flies, that suck their blood or burrow into their flesh. Since the big animals have hooves rather than claws or fingernails, they cannot easily scratch these **parasites** off their skin. Birds called oxpeckers come to their rescue. They have very strong, sharp claws on their toes for gripping on to the thick skin of animals like rhinos, giraffes and buffaloes. Oxpeckers are experts at finding pests on these animals, picking them off with their bright red or yellow beaks and eating them.

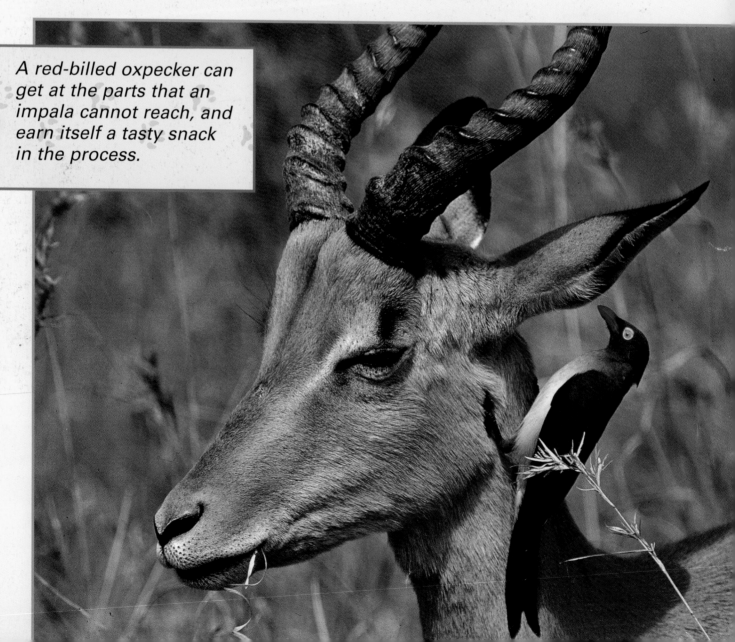

A red-billed oxpecker can get at the parts that an impala cannot reach, and earn itself a tasty snack in the process.

8

Tortoises and finches

On the Galapagos Islands in the Pacific Ocean off South America, giant tortoises enjoy the same attention. Small birds called finches hop over their skin, picking off the parasites that the tortoises cannot get at. The tortoises show they want to be groomed by raising their heavy bodies off the ground. This allows the birds to reach into every wrinkle in the tortoises' leathery skin.

This giant tortoise has no way of removing bloodsucking ticks from its skin, so it gets a little finch to do the job for it.

Another bird behaves in the same way as the Galapagos finches but in a quite different place. Out at sea, a bird called the red phalarope picks parasites off the skin of whales. The whales rise to the ocean surface, and allow the birds to poke about and rip away bloodsucking pests.

Service station

You might be surprised to learn that fish are targeted by bloodsucking **parasites** just as badly as land animals are. Some of the worst pests attach themselves to the fishes' gills, which are rows of delicate, blood-filled tubes that take in oxygen from the water. The walls of these tubes are very thin, so small bloodsuckers find them easy to attack.

On **coral reefs**, small, banded shrimps pick pests from the skin and gills of fish. These cleaner shrimps gather at special sites on the reef, and the big fish queue up, patiently waiting their turn to be picked over by the shrimps' nimble **pincers**.

This grouper would normally eat small animals like shrimps, but a cleaner shrimp can pick the grouper's teeth quite safely.

Real or fake?

Some small striped fish called cleaner wrasses do the same job. They dart all over their customers, in and out of their gills, and even into their mouths, picking off parasites and food remains with their teeth. Many of the big fish are fierce hunters, yet they never eat the small cleaners. They recognize them, partly by their behaviour, and partly by their stripes.

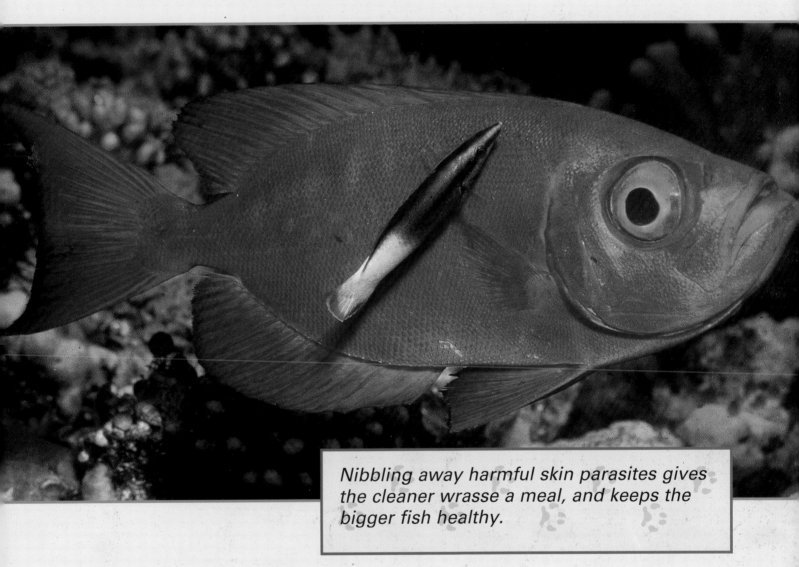

Nibbling away harmful skin parasites gives the cleaner wrasse a meal, and keeps the bigger fish healthy.

Yet some of the 'cleaners' are fakes. One small fish, a blenny called *Aspidontus*, is striped like a cleaner wrasse, and pretends to be just as useful. But when a big fish lets it get close enough, the blenny darts in and takes a bite out of it!

Poisonous protection

Corals and sea anemones are armed with thousands of tiny stings that work like poison darts. They use them to catch their **prey**, but these stings also make very good weapons to defend the corals and anemones against big fish and other enemies.

Some small fish called clown fish are not harmed by these stings. Clown fish hide among the stinging **tentacles** of big **tropical** sea anemones. The stings protect the clown fish from bigger fish, just as they protect the anemone, but it's not obvious what the anemone gets out of the arrangement. It's possible that it simply does not mind having a lodger.

Every one of these soft sea anemone tentacles is armed with hundreds of stings, but they have no effect on the little clown fish.

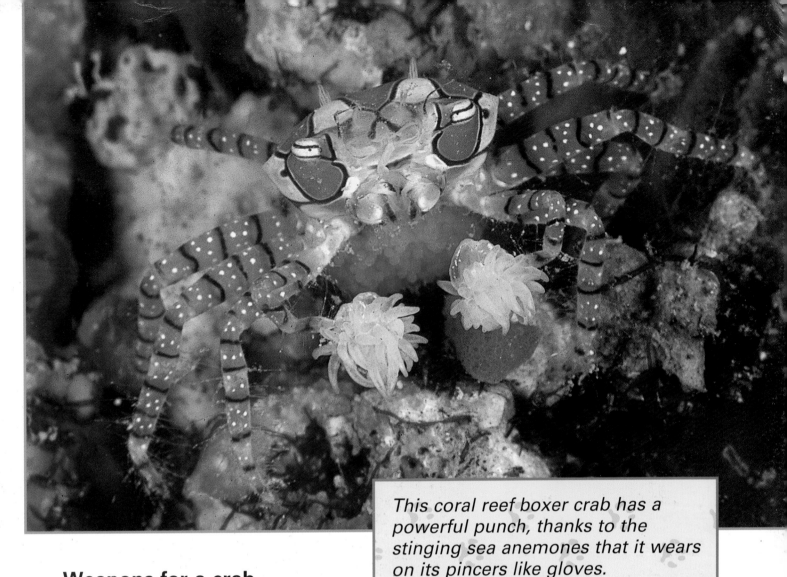

This coral reef boxer crab has a powerful punch, thanks to the stinging sea anemones that it wears on its pincers like gloves.

Weapons for a crab

The hermit crabs that live in the empty shells of sea snails sometimes carry sea anemones around with them. This is often accidental, but one **species** does it on purpose. The anemone completely covers the crab's shell like a stinging quilt, protecting the crab from its enemies in return for scraps of food. When the crab grows too big for its borrowed shell, and moves into a bigger one, the anemone moves too, with a little help from the crab.

Another species of crab attaches an anemone to each of its **pincers**. It uses them like a pair of stinging boxing gloves, to fight off its enemies. The anemones don't mind being used like this because they pick up plenty of food as the crab feeds.

Defending armies

Many insects are armed with stings and biting jaws, which they use to defend their nests. Some of the fiercest defenders are ants, and some plants use ants to protect them from plant-eating animals.

One of the most amazing is the bull's horn acacia, which lives in Central America. It grows fat thorns that are especially attractive to ants. The ants hollow them out and use them as nests. The acacia also supplies the ants with a sugary food, which they love, and a special extra-rich food that is ideal for young ants.

*Hungry acacia ants drink sugary **nectar** supplied by the acacia tree in return for their services as a defending army.*

The ants, however, need more food than this, so they also attack any insects that land on the acacia plant. Many of these insects are leaf-eaters that could strip all the leaves from the acacia, so the ants do the plant a favour by killing its enemies. They are like a defending army.

Eating the leftovers

Another tropical plant uses ants in a different way. The ant-plant lives in **mangrove** swamps. It grows high up on the branch of a mangrove tree, so it cannot take in food from the ground. Instead it has a wide, hollow stem that provides a home for ants. The ants bring their insect **prey** back to the nest and dump the leftovers in special chambers. Here, this waste rots down and supplies the plant with all the food it needs.

The weird ant-plant gets ants to keep it supplied with food, while the ants use the hollow stems of the plant as nests.

15

Aphid farm

Many plants are attacked by aphids, small bugs that feed on plants' sugary **sap**. The aphids need to eat a lot of sap to get the **protein** they need to grow and produce young. They use some of it, but get rid of the rest as a sweet syrup called honeydew.

Ants love honeydew, so whenever they find a swarm of feeding aphids, they gather the honeydew from the aphids' bodies. But the ants do more than that. They treat the aphids rather like dairy cows, and 'milk' them of honeydew in exchange for protecting the aphids from their enemies. These enemies include ladybirds and their **larvae**, and the larvae of lacewing flies and hoverflies.

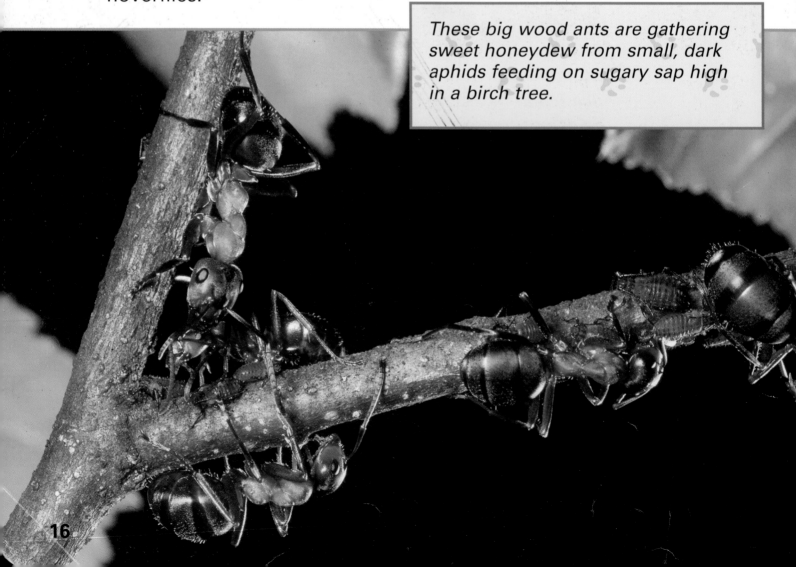

These big wood ants are gathering sweet honeydew from small, dark aphids feeding on sugary sap high in a birch tree.

Garden ants even look after aphids' eggs during the winter, so they can start new colonies in spring. If the ants end up with too many aphids, they just eat them!

Aphid shelters

The ants usually keep these killers away by fussing over the aphids. But some ants use earth and plant material to build aphid shelters at the base of plant stems. The entrances to the shelters are too small for the hunters to enter, and the ants often pick up the aphids and carry them into the shelters for protection.

Black garden ants may even carry aphids into their underground nests. They place the aphids in special chambers. There the aphids feed on the sap in growing plant roots.

The power of sunlight

Some animals are partners with tiny **algae** that are too small to see without a microscope. These algae are able to use the energy of sunlight to make sugar out of air and water. This process is called **photosynthesis**, and it is also used by all green plants. No animal can make food in this way, but if it teams up with the right algae, it can take some of the sugars that the algae produce. In exchange, it gives the algae food and somewhere to live.

The most famous of these animals are corals. A coral is a simple animal that gathers food from the water with stinging **tentacles**. Its body also contains thousands of food-making algae. The corals that form **tropical coral reefs** get most of their food from their algae, so they grow only in clear, shallow water where there is plenty of sunlight to power their tiny sugar factories.

A coral reef is like an underwater garden, growing in the tropical sunshine that gleams through the crystal-clear water.

The giant clams that live on coral reefs use the same trick. The thick, fleshy lips lining their shells are brightly coloured by the food-making algae that live in them. Like the corals, a giant clam can gather bits of food from the water, but clear, tropical seas do not have a lot of food floating in them, so the clam relies on its partnership with algae to keep it alive.

The soft lips of a giant clam are home to thousands of tiny algae, which repay the clam with sugar that they make using the energy of sunlight.

Lichen and Coral Links

The strange plant-like lichens that grow on rocks and walls use algae in the same way as corals do. A lichen is actually a mixture of a fungus and a mass of colourful algae.

A partnership between a fungus and plant-like algae allows this lichen to live on a bare rock, where neither could survive alone.

Food processors

Many **mammals** such as deer, giraffes, sheep and horses eat leaves or grass. Such foods are easy to find, but they are not ideal. Leaves contain a lot of tough material called **cellulose**. Most plant-eating animals cannot turn it into useful food.

They get help from tiny **microbes** that live in their stomachs. Most of these microbes are particular types of **bacteria** that can live in dark, airless places. The bacteria are able to break down the cellulose and turn it into sugar. They use this sugar as food for themselves, but they also produce other substances that their mammal partner can use as food. And eventually the bacteria themselves are **digested**.

Giraffes rely on the microbes in their stomachs to digest the leaves of acacia trees. Without the microbes the giraffes would starve.

Designed for grazing

All this takes time, so mammals that eat leaves or grass have big stomachs and very long **intestines** to allow the bacteria time to do their job properly. Many also have very complicated digestive systems, with different chambers for different jobs.

These leaf- and grass-eating mammals need to get their bacteria from somewhere. The young koala, which feeds on the leaves of eucalyptus trees in Australian forests, gets its bacteria from its mother. When the young koala is ready to eat leaves its mother squirts some half-digested eucalyptus out of her back end. The baby eats it, and the bacteria then start multiplying inside its own stomach.

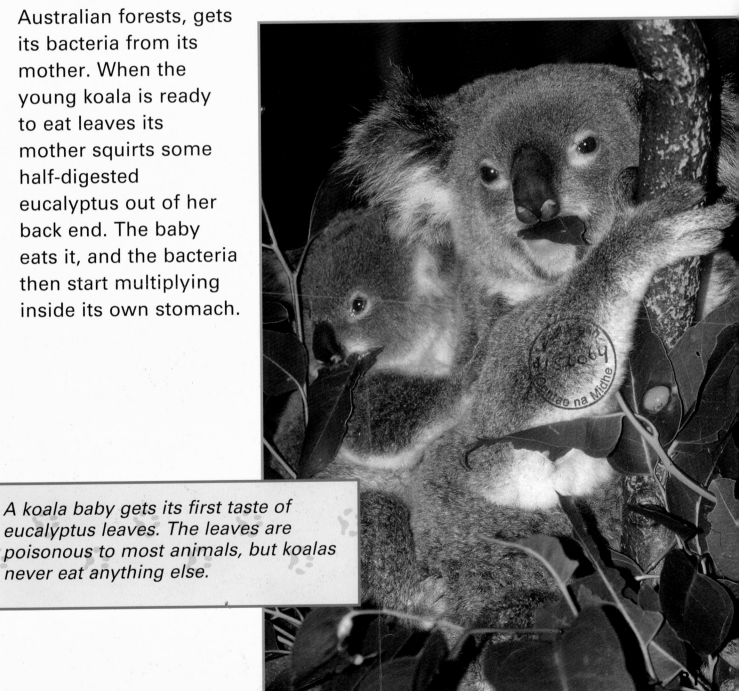

A koala baby gets its first taste of eucalyptus leaves. The leaves are poisonous to most animals, but koalas never eat anything else.

Fungus gardeners

The leaf-cutter ants that live in Central and South America are famous for the way they slice up leaves and carry the pieces back to their giant underground nests. When they get the leaves home they chew them up, but they don't actually eat them. There's no point, because the ants cannot **digest** leaves properly. This is because they do not have helpful bacteria in their stomachs to do the job. Instead, they have help in a different form.

The ants feed the chewed leaves to a type of **fungus** that lives only in their nests. Unlike the ants, the fungus can turn the leaves into useful food, so it grows well. The ants look after the fungus carefully, like tiny gardeners. They keep it aired and watered, and get rid of any pests that might attack it. And then they eat it.

This leaf-cutter ant does not eat the leaf pieces that it carries back to its nest. It feeds them to a fungus, and then eats that.

The ants do not eat all of the fungus. As it grows, the fungus produces swellings on its stems. The ants harvest these, rather like picking apples from a tree. These lumps make good food, and the ants never need anything else. They just need to keep the fungus supplied with bits of chewed leaf.

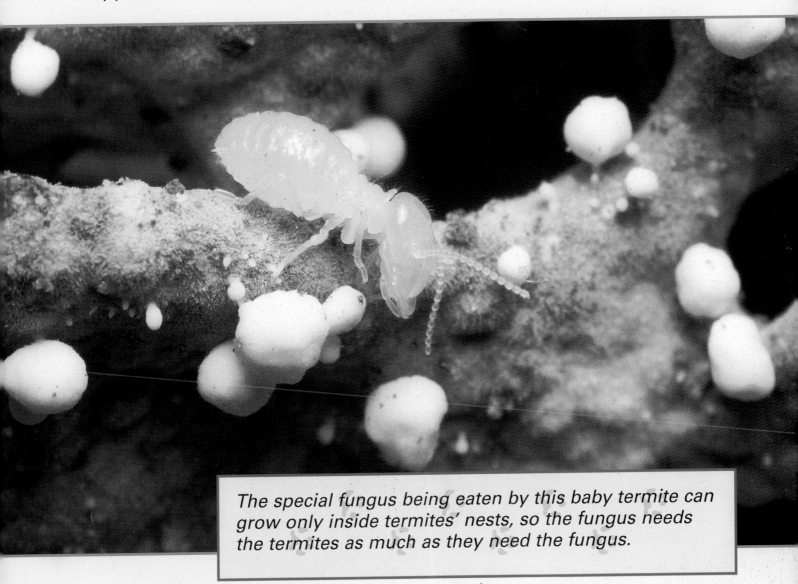

The special fungus being eaten by this baby termite can grow only inside termites' nests, so the fungus needs the termites as much as they need the fungus.

Some termites do much the same thing. Termites are rather like ants, and they too live in huge nests. Many termites are able to make a meal of almost anything, including wooden houses, but some cannot digest **cellulose**. They solve the problem by making fungus gardens inside their nests, just like leaf-cutter ants.

Sweet temptation

Flowers are very tempting to insects and birds because they contain **nectar**, a sweet food that contains lots of energy. As they feed, the animals get covered in the powdery **pollen** in the flowers. They then carry the pollen to other flowers, where it brushes off and **fertilizes** them. For this to work well, the animal has to fly straight to another plant of the same **species**. If it goes to a different type of plant, the pollen is wasted. So some plants have found ways of making animals ignore other types of flower, and just feed from theirs.

When a bumblebee lands on a snapdragon flower, its weight opens the blossom so it can get at the nectar. Other types of insect are not heavy enough, so the bumblebee prefers to feed from snapdragons because they are more likely to contain nectar. As it moves it carries pollen from one snapdragon to another.

The weight of this fat bumblebee opens the snapdragon, allowing it to get at the sweet nectar. It repays the plant by carrying its pollen from flower to flower.

Long tongues and bills

Some plants have small flowers with petals that form long tubes. Only insects with very long tongues, such as butterflies, can reach their nectar.

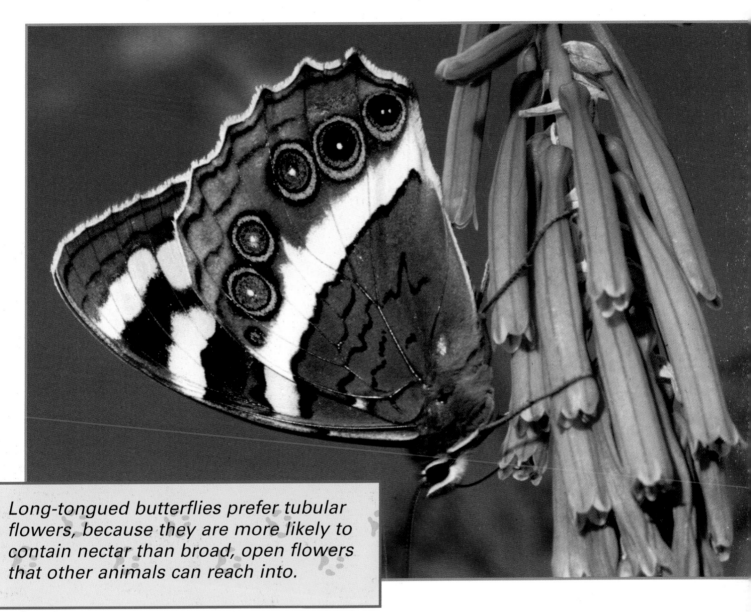

Long-tongued butterflies prefer tubular flowers, because they are more likely to contain nectar than broad, open flowers that other animals can reach into.

In **tropical** South and Central America, big tubular flowers attract long-billed hummingbirds in this way. The nectar of daturas can be reached only by the amazing sword-billed hummingbird, whose bill is as long as the rest of its body! The datura and the hummingbird are perfect partners, since each gets exactly what it wants.

Planting service

Some plants have animal partners that spread their seeds. In **tropical** forests, many trees produce seeds that are hidden inside sweet, juicy fruits. The fruits attract hungry animals such as birds, monkeys and fruit bats, which eat the soft fruits and the seeds inside them. Then they move around the forest with the seeds in their stomachs. The tough seeds pass straight through their **intestines** without being harmed. Eventually the seeds are dumped far away from their parent tree, along with a lump of manure to help them grow.

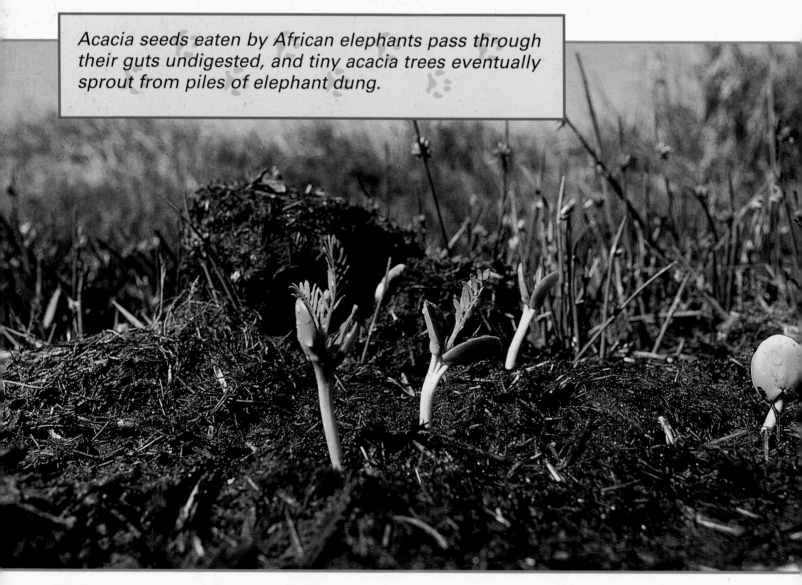

Acacia seeds eaten by African elephants pass through their guts undigested, and tiny acacia trees eventually sprout from piles of elephant dung.

Many plants that grow in the tops of forest trees are 'planted' like this. The mistletoe plants that grow in Australian forests even have a full-time partner called the mistletoe bird. The bird eats the sticky mistletoe berries, and when they emerge at its other end they are still sticky. The bird has to wipe its hind parts against rough tree bark to get rid of them, and this wedges the seeds in the places where they will grow.

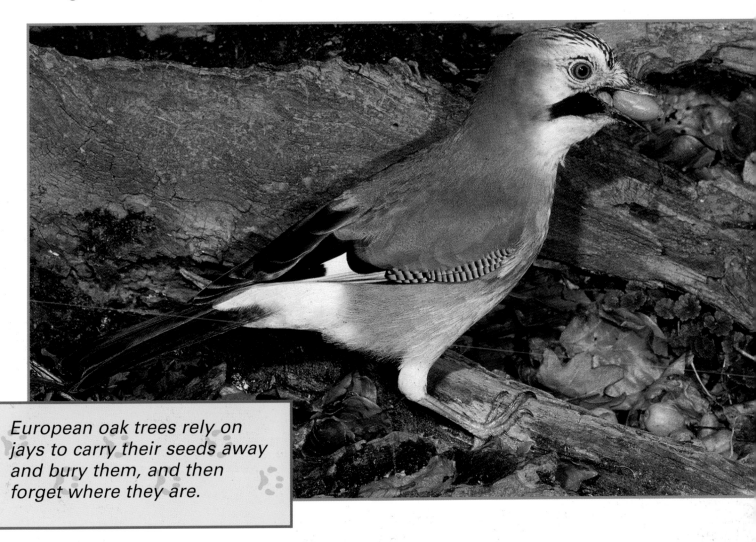

European oak trees rely on jays to carry their seeds away and bury them, and then forget where they are.

European oak trees are partners with birds called jays. The jays love eating acorns, which are the tree's seeds. As winter approaches the jays bury huge numbers of acorns to eat later, when food becomes difficult to find. A lot of the acorns are never dug up, so they sprout and become young oak trees.

Fact file

Corals can survive only in shallow, sunlit water, because their **algae** need the light to make food. If the sea level rises, the corals grow upwards to stay near the surface. Some coral reefs have been growing upwards for 50 million years, and are over a thousand metres thick.

The underground nests of leaf-cutter ants can be huge, with enough room for a grown person to stand up inside. Sometimes old nests built beneath forest roads give way beneath the weight of a truck, and the truck disappears into the hole.

Ants probably have more strange relationships with other animals than any other group of creatures. Some form weird partnerships with butterfly caterpillars, carrying them into their nests. These caterpillars eat some of the ant **larvae** in the nest, but since they also supply the ants with sweet juices, the ants do not seem to mind.

Scientists think that nearly all big animals have **microbes** in their stomachs that help them **digest** their food. We have them too. Some of these microbes are able to turn **cellulose** into sugar using a special substance which most animals cannot produce themselves. But slugs and snails can, and this allows them to digest tough plants with no trouble at all. That is why they are such pests in the garden!

The **fungus** gardens inside the nests of termites produce heat as they grow. So the termites build their nests with special air conditioning systems to stop them overheating. The air conditioning works so well that the temperature inside the nest always stays the same, at almost exactly 30 °Celsius.

Glossary

algae tiny, plant-like living things that can make food using the energy of sunlight

bacteria tiny living things that multiply by splitting in two. Some cause diseases, while others are vital to our survival.

cellulose tough fibre that gives plants their strength

coral reef colony made up of thousands of tiny animals that build a stone skeleton around their soft bodies. They share food. Corals live in shallow, sunlit seas, where their skeletons form reefs.

digest break down food into useful substances

fertilize make a seed or an egg fertile, so it grows into a plant or animal

fungus type of living thing that looks rather like a plant, but feeds more like an animal

intestines long, coiled tube leading from an animal's stomach, where its food is digested

larva (plural **larvae**) young form of an insect that does not look like its parents

mammal warm-blooded, furry animal that feeds its young on milk produced by the mother

mangrove type of tropical tree that grows on mud and water, often near the mouth of a river

microbe very small living thing that cannot be seen without using a microscope

nectar sweet, fragrant fluid produced by flowers, and eaten by insects and birds

parasite living thing that feeds on other living things while they are still alive

photosynthesis process of making sugar out of carbon dioxide (from the air) and water, using the energy of sunlight

pincers snapping claws of shrimps, lobsters and crabs

pollen fine dust produced by flowers that fertilizes other flowers so they set seed

prey animals that are attacked and eaten by other animals

protein substance made by a living thing to build its body and used as food by animals

sap fluid that carries sugar and other substances around plants

species particular type of animal

symbiosis two living things in partnership where both benefit from the arrangement

tentacles long, flexible, sensitive 'arms' of sea anemones, corals and similar animals

tropical describes hot regions of the world where the sun is directly overhead for part of the year

Index